Beavers
and Other Rodents

Concept and Product Development: Editorial Options, Inc.
Series Designer: Karen Donica
Book Author: Meish Goldish

For information on other World Book
products, visit us at our Web site at
http://www.worldbook.com

For information on sales to schools and libraries
in the United States, call 1-800-975-3250.

For information on sales to schools and libraries
in Canada, call 1-800-837-5365.

World Book, Inc.
233 N. Michigan Avenue
Chicago, IL 60601

Library of Congress Cataloging-in-Publication Data

Goldish, Meish.
    Beavers and other rodents / [Meish Goldish].
        p. cm. -- (World Book's animals of the world)
    Summary: Provides information about the physical characteristics, habits, and behavior
    of beavers and such related rodents as flying squirrels, pocket gophers, mice, and lemmings.
    ISBN 07166-1225-9 -- ISBN 0-7166-1223-2 (set)
    1. Beavers--Juvenile literature. 2. Rodents--Juvenile literature. [1. Beavers. 2.
Rodents.] I. World Book, Inc. II. Title. III. Series.

    QL737.R632 G65 2002
    599.35--dc21   2001046709

Printed in Malaysia

1 2 3 4 5 6 7 8 9 06 05 04 03 02

Picture Acknowledgments: Cover: © Erwin and Peggy Bauer, Bruce Coleman Inc.; © Pat and Tom Leeson, Photo Researchers;
© Joe McDonald, Bruce Coleman Inc.; © Kim Taylor, Bruce Coleman Inc.

© J. and D. Bartlett, Bruce Coleman Inc. 27; © Erwin & Peggy Bauer, Bruce Coleman Inc. 7, 17, 59, 61; © Jane Burton, Bruce
Coleman Collection 49, 57; © Harry Engels, Photo Researchers 23; © Mitsuaki Iwago, Minden Pictures 39; © Byron Jorjorian,
Bruce Coleman Inc. 29; © Thomas Kitchin, Tom Stack & Associates; 53; © Stephen J. Krasemann, Photo Researchers 11;
© Gordon Langsbury, Bruce Coleman Inc. 55; © Pat and Tom Leeson, Photo Researchers 21; © Joe McDonald, Bruce Coleman
Inc. 5, 4, 41, 43; © Tom McHugh, Photo Researchers 5, 35, 45, 47, 51; © Hans Reinhard, Bruce Coleman Inc. 3, 15; © Leonard
Lee Rue III, Photo Researchers 19; © Len Rue, Jr., Leonard Rue Enterprises 13; © James R. Simon, Bruce Coleman Inc. 31;
© Kim Taylor, Bruce Coleman Inc. 37; © Staffan Widstrand, Bruce Coleman Collection 33.

Illustrations: WORLD BOOK illustration by Michael DiGiorgio 25, WORLD BOOK illustration by Kersti Mack 62, WORLD BOOK
illustration by Karen Donica 9.

World Book's Animals of the World

Beavers
and Other Rodents

What's gnawing on my mind?

World Book, Inc.
A Scott Fetzer Company
Chicago

Contents

Howdy, partner. Welcome to my town!

How could you mistake me for a kangaroo?

Can you believe my weather forecasts?

What Is a Rodent?

A rodent is an animal with long front teeth called incisors. These teeth are very sharp, and they keep growing for almost the entire life of the rodent.

There are more than 2,000 species, or kinds, of rodents. Beavers are rodents. So are mice, rats, squirrels, prairie dogs, and chipmunks. Gophers and porcupines are rodents, too.

The word *rodent* comes from a Latin word that means "to gnaw" *(NAW)*. A beaver likes to gnaw, or bite, on trees. A squirrel gnaws on hard nuts. A rat can gnaw through many kinds of walls. Gnawing wears down a rodent's incisors and keeps them from growing too long.

All rodents are part of a larger group of animals called mammals. Mammals are warm-blooded animals whose babies drink their mother's milk. Mammals also have hair. Most rodents have fur.

Beaver

Where in the World Do Rodents Live?

Rodents live in almost all parts of the world. Mice and rats, for example, live on every continent except Antarctica. Porcupines live in Africa, Asia, Europe, North America, and South America. Capybaras (*KAP uh BAHR uhz*) are found only in Central America and South America.

The American beaver lives mainly in the United States and Canada. The Eurasian beaver lives in Europe and Asia.

Like many other rodents, beavers live in and near the woods. They make their homes in rivers, lakes, streams, and ponds. Often, a family of five or six beavers lives together.

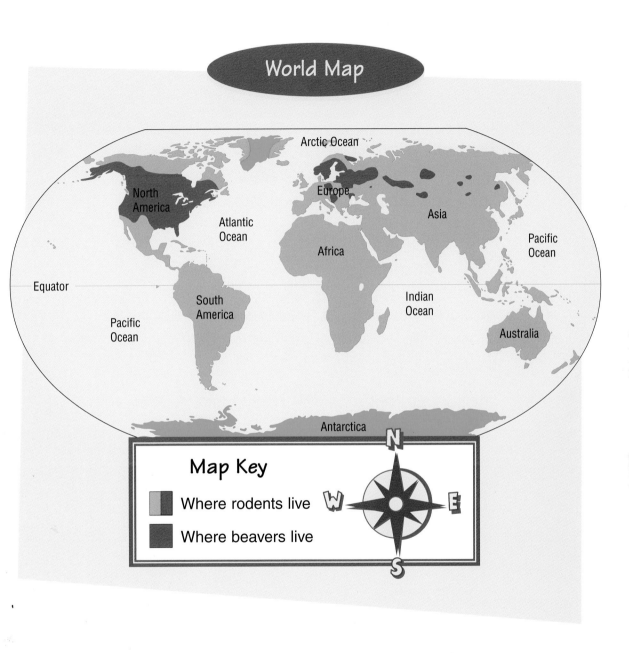

World Map

Arctic Ocean

North America

Atlantic Ocean

Europe

Asia

Pacific Ocean

Africa

Equator

South America

Pacific Ocean

Indian Ocean

Australia

Antarctica

Map Key

Where rodents live

Where beavers live

N
W E
S

9

What Makes a Beaver a Rodent?

A beaver, like all rodents, has four incisors. A beaver has two incisors in its upper jaw and two in its lower jaw. Beavers use their incisors to gnaw.

The front of each incisor has a very hard orange coating. The back of each incisor is much softer. It wears down faster than the front. As a beaver gnaws, this difference in hardness allows each incisor to form a sharp edge, like the edge of a chisel.

Incisors are not a beaver's only teeth. A beaver also has 16 back teeth that are used for chewing.

In between a beaver's front and back teeth is a long gap. In this gap are flaps of skin that actually separate the front and back of the animal's mouth. This helps a beaver gnaw wood without swallowing splinters. A beaver can also gnaw in a pond without swallowing water. If this rodent wants to eat or drink, it just opens its skin flaps!

A beaver's incisors

What Do Beavers Like to Gnaw?

Beavers love to gnaw trees. They eat the inner bark, twigs, roots, and leaves. A beaver's favorite trees are poplars, aspens, cottonwoods, willows, and birches. One acre of trees can feed a family of six beavers for more than a year!

Like most rodents, beavers are herbivores *(HUR buh vawrz)*. That means they eat mostly plants. They eat many shrubs in the spring and summer. They also like to eat water plants such as water lilies.

Beavers plan their meals carefully. In the fall, they store food for the winter. They cut trees into small pieces. Then they stick the wood in mud underwater near their homes. In the winter, they swim under the ice and eat the wood they have stored!

Beaver gnawing

How Big Is a Beaver?

The beaver is the biggest rodent in North America. An adult beaver is 3 to 4 feet (91 to 120 centimeters) long from its head to the end of its tail. The animal weighs from 40 to 95 pounds (18 to 43 kilograms).

Thousands of years ago, beavers were even bigger than they are today. Some were nearly 8 feet (2.4 meters) long. That's about as big as a grizzly bear! Scientists are not sure why beavers have become so much smaller.

A beaver's back feet are 6 to 7 inches (15 to 18 centimeters) long. Each foot has webbed toes with strong, split claws. The webbed feet work like flippers to make the beaver a strong swimmer.

Beaver

What Is Special About a Beaver's Tail?

A beaver's tail looks somewhat like a boat paddle. It is about 12 inches (30 centimeters) long and 6 to 7 inches (15 to 18 centimeters) wide. The tail has scaly skin and almost no hair.

A beaver's tail is quite useful. In the water, it helps the beaver steer while swimming. On land, the tail supports the beaver when it stands up to eat or cut down trees.

A beaver's tail also comes in handy as a storage space. It stores body fat that supplies the beaver with energy when food is hard to find. In addition, the tail stores two body oils. The beaver uses one oil, castoreum *(kas TAWR ee uhm)*, to mark its territory. It uses the other oil to waterproof its fur.

The tail serves as a defense weapon, too. If a beaver senses danger, it slaps its tail hard on the water. The loud noise warns other beavers in the area to take cover.

Beaver swimming

17

How Is a Beaver's Fur Helpful?

A beaver's fur is helpful in many ways. For example, it is so thick that it can protect the beaver from insect bites and pointy sticks.

Fur also helps a beaver in the water. A beaver can waterproof its fur by combing in its body oil with its claws. Once the fur is waterproof, it helps keep the beaver warm as it swims.

Fur keeps a beaver comfortable in cold weather, too. The fur traps body heat underneath. It acts like a blanket to keep the beaver warm, even in freezing weather.

Fur also helps a beaver stay safe. Its brown color lets the beaver blend in with trees and bushes. That way, beavers can hide from their enemies.

Beaver waterproofing
its fur

What Keeps a Beaver Busy?

Beavers seem to be at work all the time. They are often busy gnawing down trees. Beavers eat some parts of the trees and use other parts to build homes. Beavers cut trees even after they have a home and plenty of food. Scientists don't know why beavers like to do so. But one reason may be to keep their incisors from growing too long.

Cutting down a tree takes time and hard work. First, the beaver bites the trunk in two places. It keeps biting into both cuts to make them deeper. Then it pulls off pieces of wood between the cuts. After doing this many times, the tree is ready to fall. Before the tree crashes down, the beaver runs for safety, often diving into water.

After the tree falls, the beaver returns to work. It gnaws off the branches. Then it pushes, pulls, or carries the log into the water. The beaver stores some of the branches in the water for food to eat during winter. It uses other branches to build or fix its home.

20

Beaver gnawing a tree

Why Do Beavers Build Dams?

A beaver dam is a wall of sticks and stones in a stream. The dam traps water flowing downstream. Behind the dam, a pond forms. The pond is still and deep—the perfect place for a beaver home. The pond is also a place to store food and to hide from enemies.

Building a dam keeps beavers very busy. Often a whole family works together to build the dam. The beavers begin by pushing rows of sticks into the stream bed. Then they pile rocks and mud onto the sticks to weigh them down. Later, the beavers push tree branches and grass between the sticks. They add more mud so that water cannot flow through the sticks.

It usually takes two to three days for beavers to build a dam. When it is finished, the wall of sticks is high. The top of the dam rises above the water. Beaver dams can be very long, too. Most stretch between 16 and 96 feet (5 and 30 meters) across.

Beaver building a dam

What Is a Beaver Lodge?

A lodge is a home that beavers build in a pond. The lodge is made from the same materials as the dam—sticks, rocks, and mud. The top of the lodge rises 3 to 6 feet (91 to 180 centimeters) above the water. It has a shape like a cone and looks a little like a tepee.

The lodge has several underwater tunnels and entrances. All of them lead to a main indoor room, or chamber. The chamber floor is 4 to 6 inches (10 to 15 centimeters) above the water. The chamber keeps baby beavers warm and dry. It is also a place where parents dry off after bringing food to their babies.

Beavers take good care of their lodge. They add to it and fix it often. Some beaver lodges last as long as 30 years.

Beaver Lodge

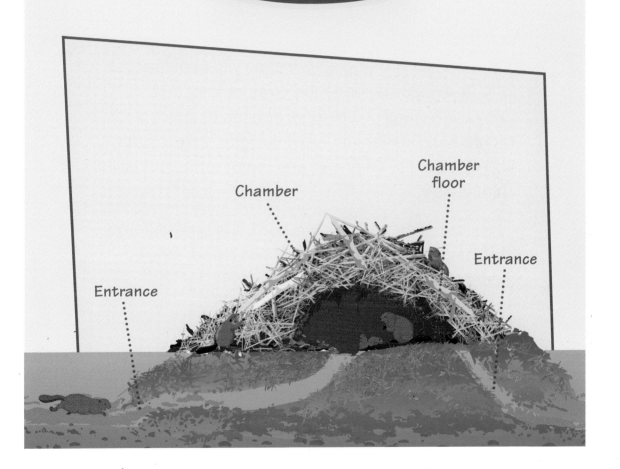

Chamber

Chamber floor

Entrance

Entrance

What Do Baby Beavers Look Like?

At birth, baby beavers look just like their parents, only smaller. Baby beavers are called *kits* or *pups*. Newborn kits are about 15 inches (38 centimeters) long from their heads to the ends of their tails. They each weigh 1/2 to 1 1/2 pounds (0.2 to 0.7 kilograms). Beaver kits have thick fur, sharp teeth, and open eyes. They can see, hear, walk, and swim immediately.

Before baby beavers are born, the other family members get the lodge ready. They work closely together to do this.

The mother carries her babies inside her body for three months before giving birth. She has two to four babies at a time. Usually they are born in April or May.

Adult beaver
with babies

What Is Life Like for Beaver Kits?

Like all mammals, baby beavers drink only their mother's milk at first. They swim for the first time inside the lodge. They're too young to waterproof their own fur, so their mother does it for them.

After one month, the kits can leave the lodge. The mother shows them how to find food and escape from enemies. The kits learn by doing what she does.

As kits grow, they play together. They wrestle and chase each other. They also dive and swim. All this exercise helps make their muscles stronger.

After one year, the young beavers are ready to start working. They cut down trees and help build and fix the dam and lodge. They also help their parents care for their newest brothers and sisters.

Young beavers live at home for about two years. Then they must go off on their own. In time, they each find a mate and build a new lodge.

28

Beaver kits

Who Are a Beaver's Enemies?

A beaver's most dangerous enemy is the otter. An otter can swim into a beaver lodge through the underwater tunnels. Inside, the otter often attacks weak and helpless beaver kits.

On land, a beaver has many more enemies. They include coyotes, wolves, foxes, and bears. Other enemies, such as hawks, eagles, and owls, may not attack an adult beaver, but they will go after the kits. A beaver keeps from danger by staying in water a lot. It comes out at night to eat or work. But even then, it stays alert for signs of enemies.

If a land enemy comes near, a beaver will slam its tail down. It does this to warn other beavers of danger. Then it hides, either by going underwater or to an escape hole it has dug on land. The hole has a tunnel that leads to water. If cornered, a beaver will fight with its sharp teeth.

Coyote chasing beaver

Is a Beaver the Biggest Rodent?

The biggest rodent in North America is the beaver. However, the beaver is not the biggest rodent in the world. That honor goes to the capybara. This animal lives in Panama and South America. It grows up to 4 feet (1.2 meters) long. It can weigh over 100 pounds (45 kilograms).

The capybara looks like a small, furry pig. It has a thick body, short legs, a flat nose, and a short tail. Like a beaver, a capybara has feet with webbed toes, and it is a good swimmer. It is sometimes called a *water pig* or a *water hog*.

The capybara lives on grassy land near lakes and rivers. Its name means "master of the grass." And it's with good reason, too. Grass is a very important part of the capybara's diet.

Capybara

When Is a "Beaver" Not a Beaver?

When it's a mountain beaver! Its name is misleading, however. A mountain beaver is not a beaver. A mountain beaver doesn't have a tail, as a beaver does. And a mountain beaver doesn't build dams, as a beaver does. But a mountain beaver is a rodent. In fact, the mountain beaver is the oldest kind of rodent in the world!

Mountain beavers are found in North America along the Pacific coast and in nearby mountains. There they roam the mountain forests. So at least the first part of their name is correct!

Mountain beavers live together in a colony, or large group. Like beavers, mountain beavers love water. They make their homes in tunnels near streams.

Mountain beaver

Can a Flying Squirrel Really Fly?

A flying squirrel does not fly the way a bird does. It cannot fly to a place that is higher than where it started. But when it leaps from a high place, it can glide more than 150 feet (46 meters) to a lower place. The animal has folded skin between its legs. After jumping, the flying squirrel stretches out this skin. The skin catches air and works like a parachute.

Most flying squirrels live in Asia, but some live in North America. These rodents make their homes in tree hollows. Flying squirrels found in North America grow to be 8 to 12 inches (20 to 30 centimeters) long. But those that live in Asia may grow to be 4 feet (1.2 meters) long!

All other kinds of squirrels hunt during the day. But a flying squirrel comes out only at night. Unlike most rodents, flying squirrels are not herbivores. They eat birds' eggs and insects, as well as berries and nuts. They also eat young birds and carrion, which is the remains of dead animals.

Flying squirrel

Which Rodents Sing a "Cheep" Song?

Chipmunks do! They sing a song that sounds like a short, shrill "cheep" that is repeated several times. Often, other chipmunks join in. Humans can hear these "songs" up to 300 feet (91 meters) away!

Besides singing, a yellow-checked chipmunk also can whistle. It makes a sharp whistle sound when it sees an enemy. Then it races away to safety. And the Alpine chipmunk can make a high-pitched call that sounds like "sweet, sweet, sweet."

Chipmunks are found in North America and Asia. They live in burrows, or tunnels, that they dig. They store seeds and nuts there to eat in winter.

Chipmunks are members of the squirrel family. Chipmunks that live in North America grow about 8 inches (20 centimeters) long. They often have light-colored stripes, bordered by black. Where do you find the stripes on the chipmunk in this picture?

Chipmunk

What Is a Woodchuck?

A woodchuck is actually the same animal as a groundhog. This rodent is one of the largest members of the squirrel family. It is about 2 feet (61 centimeters) long from its head to the end of its tail. It lives in Canada and the eastern and midwestern United States.

The woodchuck is an excellent digger. It digs a large underground tunnel. The tunnel often has several entrances and can be up to 30 feet (9 meters) long. A woodchuck will dig many small rooms that connect to the tunnel. That's some digging!

In the fall, the woodchuck digs a den where it goes to hibernate. The animal curls up in a ball and goes to sleep. It usually stays inside the den for the entire winter. In the United States, people watch for the rodent to come out of its den on Groundhog Day, February 2. Some people believe that if the animal sees its shadow on that day, there will be six more weeks of winter weather.

Woodchuck

Which Rodent Acts Like a Dog?

A prairie dog does! It isn't really a dog, but it sure behaves like one. A prairie dog wags its tail. When sitting up, it looks like a dog begging for a treat. It barks to warn other prairie dogs of danger. And baby prairie dogs are called pups!

Prairie dogs belong to the squirrel family. There are two main kinds of prairie dogs. Black-tailed prairie dogs live on the prairies of North America. White-tailed prairie dogs live in the Rocky Mountains.

Prairie dogs live together in large groups called *towns*. A town is a series of long underground tunnels that are connected to each other. A prairie dog town may have over 500 members.

Prairie dogs

Does a Pocket Gopher Have Pockets?

Yes, but not where you might expect to find them. A pocket gopher has a fur-lined pocket outside each cheek. The gopher stuffs its pockets with grass, nuts, or plant roots. Then it brings the food to its burrow. The pocket gopher stores its food there until it gets hungry.

Unlike a prairie dog, a pocket gopher likes to live alone. It keeps other gophers out of its burrow except when mating. It rarely leaves its tunnel.

A pocket gopher does keep busy, however. It digs a lot to make its burrow bigger. First, it loosens dirt with its incisors. Then it pushes the dirt away with its sharp front paws. Pocket gopher tunnels can be up to 800 feet (245 meters) long!

Pocket gopher

Does a Mouse Really Love Cheese?

A mouse in a house does love cheese—and anything else it can sink its teeth into! A mouse will eat almost any food that humans eat. That includes meat and vegetables. A mouse will also eat things that humans won't. For example, it will also eat glue, leather, paste, and soap!

A house mouse needs very little food. It tends to damage more food than it actually eats. This tiny rodent is only about 3 inches (7.6 centimeters) long, not counting the tail. It weighs only 1/2 to 1 ounce (14 to 28 grams).

The house mouse is the best-known kind of mouse. It lives wherever people live. It nests in homes, garages, or barns. But there are hundreds of other kinds of mice as well. They can be found all over the world—in mountains, fields, forests, swamps, and deserts.

House mouse

How Are Rats Different from Mice?

Rats look a lot like mice, but they are bigger. Even the smallest rats are bigger and heavier than the largest mice.

There are about 120 kinds of rats. The best-known kinds are the black rat and the brown rat. Black rats grow to 7 to 8 inches (18 to 20 centimeters) long, not counting their tails. Brown rats grow to 8 to 10 inches (20 to 25 centimeters) long, not counting their tails.

Rats are found all over the world. Brown rats and black rats nest in or near buildings. Other kinds of rats live in areas where people are not found.

Like mice, rats eat almost any kind of plant or animal. However, rats are just as likely to be eaten themselves. Most do not live more than a year. Their enemies include dogs, cats, hawks, owls, weasels, snakes, and other rats.

Brown rats

Which Rodents Hop Like Kangaroos?

Kangaroo rats, of course! They get their name because of the way they hop on their long, strong hind legs—just as kangaroos do.

A kangaroo rat is only about 15 inches (38 centimeters) long, but nearly half that length is its tail. Despite this, it can leap up to 6 feet (1.8 meters) in a single bound!

A kangaroo rat is neither a kangaroo nor a rat. It is actually a rodent in the pocket mouse family. A kangaroo rat lives in one of the deserts of the southwestern United States. Like a kangaroo, a kangaroo rat has short front legs. They don't touch the ground when the animal leaps. And while a kangaroo has a pouch in its belly, a kangaroo rat has two pouches outside its cheeks.

Kangaroo rat

Which Rodents Are Named for Their Smell?

Muskrats get their name from the strong odor they give off when mating. Do you know the smell of musk? It is used in many perfumes.

Muskrats are found in many parts of North America. They live near ponds, streams, and rivers. They make their homes by digging burrows near the water. In the winter, muskrats live in homes that they build out of plants held together with mud.

Muskrats have many things in common with beavers. Like beavers, muskrats have partially webbed feet that make them strong swimmers. They use their scaly tails to steer in the water. Muskrats also build lodges to hide from their enemies. But a muskrat has something that no beaver has—that strong smell of musk!

Muskrat

Where Do Lemmings Live?

Lemmings live in the cold, northern parts of the world. Most lemmings live in the Arctic tundra, a cold, dry area without trees in northern Alaska, Canada, Europe, and Asia. There lemmings make their homes in burrows they dig in the snow.

A lemming has no trouble staying warm in the cold. Its thick, furry coat traps body heat inside. Some species of lemmings have fur on the bottoms of their feet. The fur protects their feet from the snow and ice.

When snow falls and cold winds blow, some lemmings lie flat on the ground. The snow actually helps keep the lemmings warm. It helps block the wind and holds the warmth near their bodies. The lemmings also flip long, stiff hairs over their ears. Like earmuffs, the hairs help keep the lemming's ears warm.

Other lemmings simply crawl into their burrows to stay warm. It is much warmer there than it is out on the open tundra!

Lemming in a burrow

Who Has Babies Every Three Weeks?

A female beach vole *(VOHL)* can give birth every three weeks, or 17 times a year! Each litter usually has three to five babies. That means one female can have up to 85 baby beach voles in a single year! Other types of voles, such as bank voles, have three to five litters each year. That's a lot less than the beach vole, but it is still a lot of babies in a year.

With so many voles, you might think the world would be overrun with them. However, most of these rodents don't live for very long. Most voles live for only 8 to 13 weeks. They are killed by enemies or die from disease or lack of food.

Voles are about 5 inches (13 centimeters) long. They look somewhat like mice, and most have gray fur. Many species of voles are named for their habitats. Meadow voles live in grassy meadows. Water voles live near water. Tundra voles, like lemmings, live in the cold tundra.

Bank vole

How Many Quills Does a Porcupine Have?

A porcupine has about 30,000 quills on its back, sides, and tail. The quills are sharp, stiff hairs. A porcupine uses them for defense. If an enemy attacks, the porcupine strikes with its quilled tail. The quills from a porcupine's body also stick into the skin of an attacker if it gets too close. When the attacker pulls away, the quills stay stuck to its body. This is very painful for the attacker and can even be deadly. That's why most animals leave a porcupine alone!

Quills also help a porcupine to swim. The quills have a spongelike filling that helps the porcupine float on water. Floating in a stream or pond is a great way to enjoy a meal of water plants.

Porcupine

Are Rodents in Danger?

Nearly all rodents have natural enemies. Enemies include bears, wolves, weasels, cats, snakes, hawks, eagles, and owls.

Humans, though, cause rodents the most danger. Farmers kill rodents that damage their crops, animals, or property. Beavers and other rodents are hunted for their fur. People often kill rats that carry diseases such as typhus, rabies, and the plague.

Long ago, people trapped so many beavers that these animals nearly became extinct. Coats and hats were made with beaver fur. Today, laws in the United States protect beavers by limiting the times of year when they may be hunted. Many countries in Europe are also now importing beavers. This is helping beavers to find new habitats.

Although they always face dangers, few kinds of rodents, if any, will become extinct. Most multiply so quickly that they will be around for a long time to come.

Beaver

Rodent Fun Facts

→ A pocket gopher sees poorly and uses its tail to feel its way around its burrow.

→ Beavers usually stay underwater for 4 to 5 minutes at a time. The longest recorded time a beaver held its breath underwater is 15 minutes.

→ Some beaver dams are over 1,000 feet (305 meters) long! That's longer than three soccer fields!

→ A mountain beaver is also called a *whistler*, even though it makes no whistling sound.

→ One prairie dog town in Texas was 250 miles (402 kilometers) long and 100 miles (161 kilometers) wide. Millions of prairie dogs lived there!

→ A porcupine grows new quills after losing its old ones. The name *porcupine* comes from two French words meaning "quill pig."

Glossary

burrow A hole dug in the ground by an animal for refuge or shelter.

carrion The remains of dead animals.

castoreum An oily substance with a strong odor that is secreted by beavers.

chamber The main room in a beaver lodge.

colony A large group of animals of the same kind.

dam A wall of sticks and stones that beavers build in a stream or river to hold back water.

gnaw To bite at and wear away.

herbivore An animal that feeds mostly on grass or other plants.

hibernate To sleep through the cold months.

incisor A sharp, long front tooth.

kit The name for the young of some kinds of animals.

lodge A home that beavers build in a pond.

mammal A warm-blooded animal that feeds its young on the mother's milk.

musk A substance with a strong odor that is released by some animals.

pouch A fold of skin, shaped like a bag, that some animals have.

pup The name for the young of some kinds of animals.

quill A stiff, sharp hair or spine like the end of a feather.

rodent A type of mammal with four incisors.

town A large group of prairie dogs.

tundra A vast treeless plain in the arctic regions.

waterproof To keep water out.

webbed Having toes joined by a piece of skin.

(Boldface indicates a photo, map, or illustration.) # Index

For more information about rodents, try these resources:

The Beaver, by Sabrina Crewe, Raintree/Steck-Vaughn, 1999.
Prairie Dogs, by Emery Bernhard, Harcourt Brace, 1997.
Rodents: From Mice to Muskrats, by Sara Swan Miller, Franklin Watts, 1999.

http://beaversww.org/index.html
http://www.enchantedlearning.com/subjects/mammals/rodent/Printouts.shtml
http://www.nationalgeographic.com/burrow/index.html

Rodent Classification

Scientists classify animals by placing them into groups. The animal kingdom is a group that contains all the world's animals. Phylum, class, order, and family are smaller groups. Each phylum contains many classes. A class contains orders, an order contains families, and a family contains individual species. Each species also has its own scientific name. Here is how the animals in this book fit in to this system.

Animals with backbones and their relatives (Phylum Chordata)

Mammals (Class Mammalia)

Rodentia (Order Rodentia)

Beaver (Family Castoridae)

American beaver................................. *Castor canadensis*
Eurasian beaver .... *Castor fiber*

Capybara (Family Hydrochaeridae)

Capybara .... *Hydrochaeris hydrochaeris*

Lemmings, mice, rats, and their relatives (Family Muridae)

Black rat .... *Rattus rattus*
Brown rat .... *Rattus norvegicus*
House mouse .... *Mus musculus*
Meadow vole .... *Microtus pennsylvanicus*
Muskrat .... *Ondatra zibethicus*
Tundra vole.................................... *Microtus oeconomus*
Water vole .... *Microtus richardsoni*

Mountain beaver (Family Aplodontidae)

Mountai beaver................................ *Aplodontia rufa*

New World porcupines (Family Erethizontidae)

North American porcupine .... *Erethizon dorsatum*

Pocket gophers (Family Geomyidae)

Pocket mice and kangaroo rats (Family Heteromyidae)

Squirrels and their relatives (Family Sciuridae)

Alpine chipmunk................................ *Tamias alpinus*
Black-tailed prairie dog.......................... *Cynomys ludovicianus*
White-tailed prairie dog .... *Cynomys leucurus*
Woodchuck (Groundhog)........................ *Marmota monax*
Yellow-cheeked chipmunk .... *Tamias ochrogenys*